A BRIEF HISTORY OF CANADA

HOW THE CLASH OF FRENCH, BRITISH AND NATIVE
EMPIRES FORGED A UNIQUE IDENTITY

DOMINIC HAYNES

© **Copyright - Dominic Haynes 2021 - All rights reserved.**

The content contained within this book may not be reproduced, duplicated, or transmitted without direct written permission from the author or the publisher.

Under no circumstances will any blame or legal responsibility be held against the publisher, or author, for any damages, reparation, or monetary loss due to the information contained within this book. Either directly or indirectly. You are responsible for your own choices, actions, and results.

Legal Notice:

This book is copyright protected. This book is only for personal use. You cannot amend, distribute, sell, use, quote, or paraphrase any part, or the content within this book, without the consent of the author or publisher.

Disclaimer Notice:

Please note the information contained within this document is for educational and entertainment purposes only. All effort has been executed to present accurate, up-to-date, and reliable, complete information. No warranties of any kind are declared or implied. Readers acknowledge that the author is not engaging in the rendering of legal, financial, medical, or professional advice. The content within this book has been derived from various sources. Please consult a licensed professional before attempting any techniques outlined in this book.

By reading this document, the reader agrees that under no circumstances is the author responsible for any losses, direct or indirect, which are incurred as a result of the use of the information contained within this document, including, but not limited to, — errors, omissions, or inaccuracies.

CONTENTS

Introduction   5

1. Before the Europeans (c. 12,000 BCE - c. 1000 CE)   7
2. A Prelude of Things to Come (c.1000 - 1697)   13
3. War, La Guerre, and the Anglo-French Rivalry (1698-1791)   25
4. A Nation in Its Nascency (1792-1841)   33
5. Canada on the World's Stage (1842-1918)   43
6. What is and What is to Come (1919-2021)   51

Other books by Dominic Haynes   59
References   61

HOW TO GET A FREE HISTORY EBOOK

Would you like a free copy of a surprise history ebook?

Get free and unlimited access to the below surprise history ebook and all of my future books by joining my Fan Base.

Scan with your camera to join!

INTRODUCTION

Human conflict and collision have long driven the pace of history forward, shaping some empires while destroying others. The story of Canada as a product of a great cultural clash is not unique to the world--many nations have risen from the ashes of their forefathers' fights. Yet in Canada, the struggle for supremacy that slogged along between the Indigenous Populations, the British Empire, and the French Empire gave birth to a nation that retains the deep marks and influences of these people, despite any attempts from one group to erase or eliminate the other. Here, in this massive and resource-rich northern country, the power games of Europe landed on the North American Continent, forcing Indigenous People to engage in a fight for their survival.

Although the British Empire undoubtedly ended up dominating the prevailing culture, government, and language from the mid-eighteenth century onward, the survival of the distinct and tenacious communities of the First Nations, Inuit, and Métis, as well as the French Canadians' continued refusal to capitulate to British influence, gave rise to a blended nation that has worked to forge its own destiny separate from both its former European overlords and its aggressive southern brother and neighbor. Canada, now a powerful nation in its own right, bears both the glories and the scars of those who fought to make it what it is and what it has yet to become.

BEFORE THE EUROPEANS (C. 12,000 BCE - C. 1000 CE)

The first Canadians likely originated from a population that was either inhabiting or migrating across Beringia, a massive expanse of land that joined modern-day Siberian Russia and Alaska. Though this swath of land was plunged into the icy waters of the Bering Sea when the last Ice Age came to a close some 14,000 years ago, it is conventionally thought that this was the route through which humans made their way into the interior of the North American continent. This theory, though neat and convenient, is likely only a partial truth. It is quite plausible that many people did trek across and even populate Beringia since it would have been an existing landmass for thousands of years. However, it is probably not the only way that people arrived on the North and South American continents. In various parts of North and South America, and in Canada specifically, evidence has been unearthed that implies that humans were not only in the Americas far earlier than originally thought, but that they also inhabited the coastline.

In British Columbia, a southwestern province of Canada, archeologists have discovered evidence that supports the idea that early humans traveled down the Pacific Coast of North America by boat, utilizing the rich resources provided by the sea. A maritime migration across the Pacific Ocean is equally probable, but it is important to remember that no one knows with full certainty and authority how people came to the American continents. Research is ongoing, and the full truth may never be uncovered. There is also a far shakier theory, known as the Solutrean Hypothesis that suggests the earliest Americans came to the continent via an Atlantic maritime route. There is some evidence to support this, but most scholars agree that the Bering Land Bridge Migration and the Pacific maritime route are the more believable and supported theories.

However they arrived, the point is that they did come and settle the land long before even the earliest Europeans arrived on Canadian shores. There are three classifications the present-day Canadian government uses to refer to the Indigenous populations within their nation: the First Nations, the Inuit, and the Métis. The First Nations are a massive group of Indigenous people who populated most of Canada and the northern United States. They are often placed into different geographical categories, but it is crucial to remember that each tribe within the First Nations has its own culture, history, and identity. It is incorrect to view them as one people since they never united as one people and never saw themselves as a monolith.

The Woodland First Nations made their home in the thickly forested land of eastern Canada and consisted primarily of nomadic hunters and trappers or more sedentary agricultural settlements. Tribes like the Algonquin relied more heavily on hunting and trapping and maintained smaller groups, while the agricultural bounty of the Iroquoian (Haudenosaunee) Nation allowed them to form a large confederation with complex political systems. The Iroquois Confederation was the first group of Indigenous people to make sustained contact with Europeans. The Woodland First Nations include the Mi'kmaq, Huron-Wendat, and Kanienkehaka (Mohawk) nations, among many others.

Moving west into the flat, prairie provinces of Manitoba, Alberta, and Saskatchewan, the Great Plains First Nations were primarily migratory peoples that followed buffalo herds. Including the Blackfoot,

Ojibwa, and Cree among others, the Plains First Nations often organized their social structure around a chief, and though independent, would frequently trade and interact with one another, and with the nations along the Pacific Coast.

In the high, craggy reaches of the Rocky and Cascade mountain ranges the semi-nomadic Plateau First Nations formed seasonal villages that were easily movable when necessary. Plateau First Nations like the Athapascan and Ktunaxa relied on the rivers that coursed through the area for both food and transportation.

Remembered for their colorful totem poles, the Pacific Coast First Nations were excellent fishermen who developed a complex political system and social stratification. Tribes like the Haida and Nootka had a hereditary noble class, a common class, and a slave class. Slaves were either bought or captured in war, and a person's nobility often hinged on their blood ties to the chief. Some of the Pacific Coast First Nations' trading partners in the Plains First Nations adopted their intricate social structure in their own tribes.

To the north, where the winters were harsher and food scarcer, the First Nations of the Yukon and Mackenzie River Basins relied on hunting caribou. Leadership in the groups, rather than hereditary and concrete, would change depending on what was needed at any given time.

Even further north, into the inhospitable Canadian Arctic, the Inuit subsisted off of whales, seals, and caribou. These hunters and gatherers would move in seasonal groups that tended to be larger during the winter months and smaller during summer hunts. They were the last group of Canadian Indigenous people to make sustained contact with the Europeans, and thus were the last to change their traditional ways of life. Their territory stretches through the Canadian Arctic to Alaska in the west and Greenland in the east.

Though this short overview hardly does justice to the complexity, color, and individuality of the First Nations and Inuit, it should be apparent that there was a great deal of diversity, life, and human presence in Canada long before the arrival of any European. Their medicinal knowledge, agricultural techniques, hunting and trapping techniques, and knowledge of the topography of their lands made it possible for the Europeans who eventually landed in Canada to survive. Much of the knowledge that white settlers acquired in their conquest of Canada was imparted to them by their contact with and observation of the First Nations and the Inuit.

These people still exist today and have been on the receiving end of brutal treatment at the hands of their white contemporaries over the centuries. While Canada is now slowly coming to terms with the cultural genocide that took place, it is important to acknowledge the history of pain and suffering. First Nations and Inuit have left valuable, indelible marks on Canadian history and continue to contribute to the forward progress of the nation to this day.

There is a third group of Indigenous people that have yet to be discussed: the Métis. They have their own distinct history and cultural contributions, but being of mixed Native and European ancestry, they will be addressed later in the text.

2

A PRELUDE OF THINGS TO COME
(C.1000 - 1697)

Sometime around the dawn of the eleventh century, the earliest Europeans stumbled upon the shores of Canada. The Norse people had been slowly pushing westward from their native homeland of Scandinavia, settling in Iceland in the ninth century and then Greenland during the tenth. From there, it is thought that they would send out expeditions that would have roved up and down the coast of Baffin Island, Newfoundland, and Labrador. Though Norse sagas tell of several expeditions into Canada, which they called Vinland, the only solid archeological evidence of a Norse settlement in Canada is at L'Anse aux Meadows on the northern tip of Newfoundland.

There is little evidence that suggests there was any kind of working relationship between the Indigenous people of Canada and the Norse settlers, but L'Anse aux Meadows was populated by First Nations people both before, during, and after the Norse presence. Additionally, the Norse were aware of the Indigenous people of both Canada and Greenland, whom they referred to as *Skraelings*. Contact between Indigenous tribes and the Norse are described in a wide manner of ways throughout the sagas, ranging from amicable to cautious to downright violent.

Though the research is ongoing, the Norse occupied an area of Newfoundland and Greenland for an undetermined period and likely left due to either a dwindling population, hostility from the native inhabitants, or an inability to cope with the exceedingly cold winters. Starting around the 12th century, scholars believe that the climate began to grow increasingly colder as the earth descended into a Little Ice Age. Though this does not seem to have affected the Inuit, who feasted on seals and did not suffer a setback during the Little Ice Age, the winter slowly became untenable for the Norse settlers. After a particularly harsh winter in 1355, the Norse abandoned their settlement in Greenland, their last colony in the New World.

Sometime between the Norse expeditions into Newfoundland and Labrador and the later arrival of other European interlopers, a powerful political entity was coalescing in the Woodlands First Nations. Though the exact date is unknown--some date it as far back as 1142 and others as recently as the mid to late fifteenth century--five nations came together in the areas known today as upstate New York and southeastern Canada. These nations, the Onondaga, Kanienkehaka (Mohawk), Cayuga, Oneida, and Seneca, came together to form the Iroquois or Haudenosaunee Confederation. Becoming one of the most powerful political arbiters in North America, these five nations banded together at the urging of a Seneca man named Hiawatha and a Huron-Wendat man living among the Kanienkehaka named Dekanawida (the Great Peacemaker). The nations pledged to accept the Great Law of Peace, rather than continue to fight one another. They were an extremely important political institution before the arrival of European settlers and continued to be a political force during the early days of the United States and Canada. Their involvement in both trade and in war shaped the future of the North American continent, and it is thought that their democratic and constitutional ideas had an impact on the formation of the governments of both the United States and Canada.

As the First Nations and Inuit continued to progress onward in their daily lives, across the Atlantic in Europe, a storm was brewing. Europe had long been embroiled in power plays and wars on its own continent, and now, thanks to the rapidly developing maritime technology, the Age of Exploration was dawning. Trade between Asia and Europe had been well established since the days of the Roman Empire, but in 1453, the Ottoman Empire closed the Silk Road, an overland trading route between Asia and Europe. Eager to resume trade with Asia, Spain sent Christopher Columbus across the Atlantic in search of an oceanic route to Asia. Unaware of the presence of North and South America, when Christopher Columbus landed in the Caribbean in 1492, he initially believed he had landed in India. Hence the modern moniker of West Indies as a collective term for the Caribbean islands.

England, eager to keep up with Spain, sought their own representative to sail the Atlantic in search of Asia. John Cabot, an Italian sailing under the commission of the English King Henry VII, made landfall in Canada in 1497, a few years after Columbus in the Caribbean. He too, initially believed he had reached Asia's northeastern shore and claimed the land for England. The exact site of his landfall is unknown, but it is believed to be somewhere around Newfoundland or Labrador. Though he never formally established any settlement in Canada, his initial presence was crucial to the English Crown's later claims to the land.

Once it became clear that these places discovered by Cabot and Columbus were not Asia, but a new land entirely, European superpowers engaged in a furious maritime race, eager to seize a slice of the New World's wealth for themselves. Though many often think of the English and French empires when it comes to Canada, the Portuguese first attempted to colonize and claim the land after Cabot. Their interests had previously lain in India and Africa, but with Spain moving into the New World, the Portuguese were eager to keep up. In 1499 João Fernandes explored Newfoundland and Labrador, and in 1501, his countryman Gaspar Corte-Real followed. Though no formal colony was ever established, they kept up a fishing presence in the area, happy to capitalize on the plentiful cod. There are also Portuguese place names in the area as well as Portuguese maps from the time that include portions of Newfoundland and Labrador, suggesting that their presence in Canada was somewhat significant for a time.

The first French arrival in Canada came some thirty years later when Jacques Cartier sailed up the St. Lawrence River. Claiming the land for the King of France, he also dubbed the place Canada, thanks to a misunderstanding of the Iroquois language. *Kanata* in Iroquois simply means village. Though no permanent French settlement resulted from Cartier's three voyages into Canada, he gave the country many of its French place names and laid the groundwork for the French Crown's claim to the land.

Almost a century after their first foray into Canada, England, now under the control of Henry VII's granddaughter Elizabeth I, returned once again. In 1583, Humphrey Gilbert landed around present-day St. Johns and eagerly claimed Newfoundland for his queen. His unfortunate death at sea waylaid English colonization in North America for another twenty or so years.

Finally, at the dawn of the seventeenth century, Europe got a firm toehold in the North American continent. The English put down roots to the south in what would become the United States with the founding of Jamestown, Virginia in 1607, while the French were the first to settle in Canada; establishing Port-Royal (the colony would later be known as Acadia) in 1605. France continued to expand into Canada, with Samuel de Champlain dubbing the land "New France" and founding the city of Quebec as its capital in 1608.

Though English interest in Canada continued and explorers like Martin Frobisher, Henry Hudson, and William Baffin had continued to probe the northern reaches of the land, leaving English place names along the way (Hudson Bay, Baffin Bay, Baffin Island), they lagged behind the French in establishing a permanent colony. Two years after the founding of Quebec, the English finally inaugurated their first permanent Canadian colony at Cuper's Cove (now Cupids) in Newfoundland. The English began to settle and expand to the north and south of the French, who were continuing their colonial growth to the south and west along the St. Lawrence River with the founding of Trois-Rivières in 1634 and Fort Ville-Marie (Old Montreal) in 1642.

The French and the English were old rivals, and the theatre of a new land did little to change that. Their animosity continued, unabated, with North America frequently becoming a bone of contention between the two crowns. The resources of Canada were rich indeed, and both French and English interests were eager to capture a monopoly on the most sought-after item of the day: fur. Indigenous populations had utilized the furs of the native animals for clothing, blankets, and shelter over the years, but the advent of European demand for North American fur kicked the trapping and trading into a fever pitch. French fur traders leaned heavily on their relationship with First Nations people in the Great Lakes region to secure a steady supply of fur, particularly the prized beaver pelts.

In the middle of the 1600s, two French fur traders, Médard Chouart de Groseillies and Pierre-Esprit

Radisson, thought that it made good sense for a fur trading company to access the fur available in the interior of Canada via Hudson Bay. They proposed their idea to the French, but were largely ignored and unsupported. Instead of abandoning the idea, the two appealed to the English monarchy and happened to catch the interest of King Charles II's cousin, Prince Rupert. Rupert, in turn, convinced the king, and in 1670, the Hudson's Bay Company was given a royal charter. This granted the company a trading monopoly on the land and rivers surrounding the Hudson Bay, an area subsequently named Rupert's Land.

The wealth and power accrued by the Hudson's Bay Company certainly increased English influence over Canada, and it also increased English interest in Canada, as it was now an important piece of the colonial economy. The arrival of English people and business interests in the interior of the continent had untold consequences for the Indigenous inhabitants of the area. The fur trade between English and Indigenous communities tied the two economies tightly together, and demand for and reliance on English commodities and goods among the Indigenous people spiked. As different Indigenous nations competed with one another to become the better trading partner for their new European neighbors, conflict among these nations increased. Furthermore, the inadvertent introduction of unfamiliar European diseases like smallpox decimated the native populations.

The new dominance of the Hudson's Bay Company threatened French economic interests in the area, and the two nations continually squabbled over who had the rights to trap and trade, especially in the southern portions of Rupert's Land. Naval and land battles frequently broke out between the two empires until the 1713 Treaty of Utrecht forced France to accept England's claim to the Hudson Bay. Though largely destructive to all the inhabitants of Canada, the skirmishes between France and England did allow the Indigenous people to pit the two European kingdoms against one another from time to time and secure the highest possible prices for their furs.

It is impossible to discuss the fur trade in Canada without acknowledging the Métis people. It should be noted that the use of the term "Métis" or "métis" has heavy historical weight, and the definition can depend on who one is speaking with and what one believes. Traditionally, métis with a lowercase "m" refers to people of mixed Indigenous and French ancestry, or more frequently today, a person of mixed Indigenous and European ancestry. When utilizing the term "Métis" with a capital "M," it is often referring to a specific community of people of mixed European and

Indigenous descent that coalesced in the Red River region of Western Canada during the early 19th century. A simple way of thinking of it is that "métis" refers to a racial category while "Métis" refers to a specific socio-political group.

Either way, the fur trade in the interior of Canada certainly led to a rise in culturally mixed marriages and relationships resulting in mixed children. This began primarily in the Great Lakes region with French trappers and traders during the rise of the French fur trade in the seventeenth century. The mixed population at the time did not refer to themselves as métis, and instead favored terms like bois brûlés (burnt wood) or chicot.

As is the case for large swaths of European history, France and England found themselves on opposing sides of yet another war that spilled across the world's continents. The Nine Years' War (1688-1697) broke out between France and a European coalition that included the English empire. It is also referred to as the War of the Grand Alliance or the War of the League of Augsburg, but in North America, the conflict is primarily known as King William's War with the primary parties being the French empire, French colonists, and the Indigenous people of the Wabanaki Confederacy against the English empire, English colonists, and the

Haudenosaunee/Iroquois Confederacy. Primarily due to disagreements about where the boundaries between French and English possessions truly lay, tensions between English and French colonists in New England, New France, and Newfoundland had been mounting for some time. Additionally, trade disagreements between the French and the Haudenosaunee Confederacy had soured their relationship.

After multiple naval and land battles in and around the Hudson Bay, Quebec, New York, New England, Acadia, and Newfoundland, the Treaty of Ryswick in 1697 simply reverted all the colonial borders to where they had been at the start of the war. Notably, during the war, English colonists out of Massachusetts Bay had been able to seize the French possession of Port-Royal in Acadia, but the French colonists had successfully repulsed them at Quebec. This first Battle of Quebec in 1690 was the first time, but certainly not the last, that Quebec would be forced to defend itself.

3

WAR, LA GUERRE, AND THE ANGLO-FRENCH RIVALRY (1698-1791)

The peace did not last long. A short five years later, the colonies of France and England were plunged into another conflict, Queen Anne's War (1702-1713), which is commonly viewed as the North American theatre of the War of Spanish Succession (1701-1714). With England's victory, France slowly began to lose its grip over its territories in Canada. The aforementioned Treaty of Utrecht in 1713 handed over all French claims to Acadia (now Nova Scotia), Newfoundland, and much to the Hudson's Bay Company's delight, any and all claims to Rupert's Land.

Unfortunately for all parties involved, the Treaty of Utrecht did not bring an end to the territorial conflict between the two parties. With the French maintaining Prince Edward Island (Ile St-Jean) and Cape Breton (Ile

Royal), they continued to insist on maintaining a claim to Acadia, and the Acadians were eager to thwart any British attempts to gain control of the region. Furthermore, Indigenous tribes who had allied themselves with the French, like the Mi'kmaq, were not eager to fall in line behind the British Crown. Indigenous people and their rights to their ancestral lands were often forgotten in the sweeping European treaties that allowed large chunks of land to simply change European hands. This was exceedingly detrimental to the Indigenous people in the long run and helped to further later injustices in the histories of both the United States and Canada.

Tensions in the region never ceased, and the differences in religion between the French Catholic inhabitants of Acadia and their new Protestant British leaders did little to ease the friction. A short skirmish known as King George's War (1744-1748) did not resolve any territorial disputes between the two. On their remaining small island holdings, French leaders began to construct a series of forts and bases. The English answered by building their nearby bases at Halifax and Fort Lawrence.

In the 1750s, France began to push southward from their holdings in New France into the Ohio River Valley. This brought them into direct conflict with

English settlers who were pressing westward from the British colonies along the Atlantic coast. Once again, citing conflicting territorial claims, differences in religion, and general hatred for one another, the English and French empires plunged the world into another global conflict. The Seven Years' War (1754-1763), known as the French and Indian War in North America, was fought in North America between French and English troops and colonists, with the Wabanaki Confederacy, the Huron-Wendat, Shawnee, Ottawa, Ojibwe, and Abenaki tribes fighting with the French and the Haudenosaunee/Iroquois Confederacy, the Catawba Nation, the Cherokee Nation, the Delaware/Lenape, and Mohican tribes working with the British. The Kanienkehaka (Mohawk) people located in upstate New York supported the British, while their brothers north of the St. Lawrence River in Canada allied with the French.

Meanwhile, north in Acadia, the British governor of the region grew increasingly suspicious of the Acadians' loyalty after noting an Acadian militia defending the French Fort Beauséjour. In 1755, he insisted the Acadians swear an oath of allegiance to Great Britain. When they refused, he had them imprisoned and subsequently deported. Many Acadians drifted south to the French stronghold of Louisiana where they became known as "Cajuns."

Initially, the French seemed to be faring well in the conflict, but when English politician (and later Prime Minister) William Pitt realized the gravity that a victory in North America could hold for the British Empire, he became single-minded in his mission to defeat the French. His financing enabled the British to turn the tide of the war. After a series of British victories at Louisbourg, Fort Frontenac, Fort Duquesne, and Quebec, the French lost their final Canadian holding when the British took Montreal in 1760.

With the Treaty of Paris in 1763, the whole of Canada was delivered into the hands of the British Empire. There were massive ramifications on the Indigenous people who were once again left out of the European treaty. With the French gone, there was no larger power to stop the British colonists from slaking their desire to expand westward. Additionally, the British Crown cared little to protect the rights of the Indigenous tribes from their colonists, particularly the ones who had aligned themselves with the French.

With the French trappers and traders gone in Canada, the fur trade fell squarely into British hands. The colony of New France was renamed Quebec, while the smaller French island holdings were now incorporated into the colony of Nova Scotia. Unsurprisingly, a changing of names and flags did little to realign the hearts of the French colonists who now found themselves subjects of the British Crown. Aside from language, laws, and culture, there was the thorny issue of religion. Being Catholic in the British Empire was generally not accepted, since the nation had first turned away from the Catholic Church during the reign of King Henry VIII some two hundred and fifty years earlier.

Colonists of English descent were suspicious of their new French counterparts and argued that their Catholicism robbed them of a say in their government, while colonists of French descent argued that they should not have to abandon their entire heritage and belief system because territory had changed hands. Eventually, the Quebec Act passed in 1774 that allowed for the free practice of Catholicism as well as traditional legal practices; the French colonists practiced a semi-feudal system known as the seigneurial system. This allowed the new French subjects of the British Crown to retain a large part of their religious and cultural identity and is likely one of the reasons modern-day French Canada retains such a singular identity from the rest of the nation. The Quebec Act provided some relief for the French colonists, but it would not put to rest all the disagreements between the French and the English colonists.

To the south, consequences from the French and Indian War continued to ripple out. The British Crown had attempted to find peace with the Indigenous populations and barred its colonists from moving west past the Appalachian Mountains. The colonists' desire to spread west coupled with the heavy taxes the British government had levied to pay their substantial war debts resulted in the American Revolution (1775-1783). Hoping that they could convince the French-speaking Canadiens to join their cause against the British Empire, the American Continental Army marched north, invading Quebec in 1775. Though it was not a bad idea, in theory, the French Canadiens were largely satisfied with the provisions laid out for them in the Quebec Act. There was simply not enough motivation for them to engage in war after nearly a century of conflicts between France and Great Britain in the area. The Americans ultimately failed in Canada, but went on to defeat Great Britain in the end.

Eager to seize whatever advantage they could, the British Empire guaranteed freedom to any Black enslaved person who sided with the British against the Americans. This resulted in a wave of migration north into Canada, with many settling in Nova Scotia and establishing a community of free Black Canadians. After the American victory in 1783, a border between the new United States and the British Empire was drawn, and another wave of migrants flowed into Canada from the United States. This time, it was white loyalists to the British Crown who feared retribution from their patriot neighbors. With so many new English speakers flooding into Quebec, the language, laws, and customs of French Canada felt exceedingly foreign and uncomfortable.

The British government had just suffered a heavy blow with the loss of their American colonies and was desperate to keep conflict at bay within their Canadian holdings. The Constitutional Act of 1791 was the British government's attempt to keep both their English and French-speaking subjects happy. It divided the colony of Quebec into two pieces, Upper (southern Ontario) and Lower (southern Quebec) Canada. In Upper Canada, Protestantism was practiced, and English laws, customs, and institutions reigned. Meanwhile, Lower Canada maintained the Catholic faith as well as French laws, customs, and institutions. Even though it was clear that the Anglo-Canadians were becoming economically and politically dominant, the French Canadiens were pleased to have their own land, seemingly separate from the rest. For a brief time, the British government managed to pacify both Anglo and French Canadians.

4

A NATION IN ITS NASCENCY
(1792-1841)

Though the Hudson's Bay Company had maintained a degree of a monopoly over the Canadian fur trade since the French cessation of their rights to Rupert's Land after Queen Anne's War (The War of Spanish Succession, 1701-1714), by the end of the 1700s, another company, the North West Company had become a viable threat. During the American Revolution, the British had attempted to cut off the supply of munitions to the American Colonists through a trade embargo in the Great Lakes region. Through an unintended consequence of the embargo, trading licenses were refused to individual fur traders in Montreal. It became clear that the individual traders could have more power and influence over government, and by extension, their own fates, if they became a united front. By 1783, nine different small trading groups had banded together to form the North West Company, a massive fur trading company that operated across the North American continent and directly defied the Hudson's Bay Company's royal charter.

In contrast to the more sedentary operations of the Hudson's Bay Company, the North West Company achieved their profits and success by being constantly on the move, mostly working to the west of Rupert's Land. The nature of their work put many French-Canadian traders affiliated with the North West Company in close contact with the people of the Plains and Pacific Coast First Nations, and many fur traders married Indigenous women, particularly women of the Ojibwa, Cree, and Salteaux tribes. These women were valuable companions, diplomats, and sources of knowledge for their European husbands. Their children, exposed to both European and Native First Nations cultures, became known as the Métis, a French word that loosely translates to "mixed" or "half-breed." The Métis were introduced to and practitioners of both French Catholic and Indigenous religious traditions, and developed a distinctly blended way of life in and around the Red River Valley of central Canada. By supplying the transient North West Company employees with pemmican (a kind of dried meat paste) as well as cultivating crops and hunting local buffalo, the Métis developed a strong economy and a flourishing settlement.

Hudson's Bay Company was certainly not enthralled to have a rival working within the lands that were supposed to be theirs by royal decree, and an opportunity to undermine the North West Company's operations soon presented itself. Thomas Douglas, Lord Selkirk, a Scottish man who had come of age during the Jacobite Rebellion and subsequent Highland Clearings in Scotland during the mid-1700s, was eager to establish a new homeland for the scores displaced Scots. After becoming a majority shareholder in the Hudson's Bay Company in 1811 and guaranteeing that a percentage of his colonists would work for the Hudson's Bay Company, he managed to secure a massive tract of land from the company the following year. This large bit of land that he named Assiniboia happened to be in the Red River Valley, disrupting the current settlements of Métis people and smack in the middle of the North West Company's route into northwestern Canada.

Selkirk's colony had an incredibly rough start, and in an attempt to ration the food supplies in the area, the governor outlawed the export of pemmican. This coupled with an earlier ban on buffalo hunting within the colony's boundaries and the outright refusal of the

Assiniboia colonists to recognize the Métis claim to the land became a direct attack on the Métis way of life. The North West Company and their Métis allies soon decided that Assiniboia needed to be dissolved, and hostilities between the colonists (many of whom were employed by the Hudson's Bay Company) and the North West Company and Métis began to escalate.

At the Battle of Seven Oaks in 1816, twenty-one colonists were killed by Métis hunters employed by the North West Company; Selkirk responded by seizing the North West Company's nearby Fort William. The tensions continued, with both the North West Company and Hudson's Bay Company seeking sovereignty over the Canadian fur trade, but in the end, the Hudson's Bay Company was more financially sound. Able to outlast the costly skirmishes that economically damaged their competitor, the North West Company gave in and merged with Hudson's Bay Company in 1821. With the destructive rivalry and feud at an end, the Red River Colony was able to finally prosper economically, and the Métis population continued their way of life in the region.

Back to the east, there was trouble once again on Canada's southern border. Anglo-American relations had stayed rancorous in the years following the American Revolution, and the United States had finally been goaded into war with the British over the repeated violations of American maritime rights. The War of 1812 (1812-1815), sometimes viewed as a second war for American independence, sparked fears in British-occupied Canada that the Americans meant to unify the whole of North America under their auspices.

The majority of the War of 1812 was fought along the United States-Canadian border, with American forces invading the British colony several times during the war. One particular invasion that resulted in the Battle of Beaver Dams (June 24, 1813) has been largely mythologized in Canadian history. Laura Secord, the wife of a merchant and Canadian militiaman James Secord, was living in the American-occupied town of Queenston (present-day Ingersoll, Ontario) and happened to overhear American plans to surprise the British forces at Beavers Dam. Secord then apparently trekked some nineteen miles (thirty kilometers) from Queenston to intercept Irish soldier James FitzGibbon and inform him of the Americans' intentions. Thanks to Secord's warnings, the British were able to ambush the Americans at Beaver Dams and provide a decisive British victory.

The extent of Secord's involvement is in question, as is the credit given to the British forces. First Nations and Métis warriors were crucial to the defense of the Canadian border, and Indigenous scouts' reports certainly assisted the British in thwarting the Americans' surprise attack. Furthermore, the Kanienkehaka (Mohawk) Tribe's guerrilla tactics against the Americans at the Battle of Beaver Dams were pivotal in delivering victory to the British.

The Treaty of Ghent at the end of the War of 1812 returned all territories and borders to the status they had held before the war, and the War of 1812 is often classed as "the war that nobody won." However, the conflict continues to hold historical significance for the North American continent. It ended the British dream of regaining any territory in their lost colonies, it proved to the young American nation that they were capable of defending their borders, and it shaped a burgeoning sense of Canadian identity. Many of the soldiers who fought and died in the war were Canadian citizen-soldiers rather than seasoned British regulars, which meant it was Canadians who fought off an invading force, not their massive and militaristic colonial mother.

The Treaty of Ghent marked a new era in Anglo-American relations, and by extension, Canadian-American relations. Gone were the days of aggression at the border, and a series of pacts between Great Britain and the United States helped to birth a lasting friendship between the two nations. The 1817 Rush-Bagot Agreement demilitarized the navies patrolling the Great Lakes while the Convention of 1818 established the western Candian-U.S. border along the forty-ninth parallel, where it still resides today.

It became clear at the close of the War of 1812 that Canada was developing a singular identity, and the people felt less and less connected to the monarch across the sea. In the early days of Canadian settlement, many of the incoming Europeans were farmers and fur traders, focused on their economic futures and what the land might be able to provide for them. However, as the colony continued to grow and prosper, the developing middle class grew more and more displeased with the authoritarian nature of their government. Provinces were run by crown-appointed governors who often came from wealthy British families. Parliaments were nominal or nonexistent. Many Canadians, having grown a sense of separateness from their mother country over the years, were interested in having a government that reflected their values and wishes.

As Canada moved into the 1830s, political turbulence was mounting. Several factions in different areas of Canada began to mount insurrections with differing levels of intensity. Some just wanted to reform the current government while others wished to break away from Great Britain completely, showing some interest in joining the United States. In Lower Canada (present-day Southern Quebec), the unrest was fomented by Jean-Louis Papineau and a moderate faction of French-Canadian nationalists. With reasonable requests--like more control over the colony's revenue and calling for a more responsible government that represented the colonists--shot down by the British government, more extreme French-Canadian nationalists began calling for armed conflict. Eventually, violence broke out in late 1837, and the relationship between the majority French-Canadian and minority Anglo-Canadian people who populated Lower Canada became terse and unpleasant.

The disorganized French-Canadian rebels were quickly put down by the combined effort of British regulars and Anglo-Canadian volunteers. Papineau and his followers temporarily fled to the United States, returning for a second uprising a year later. This too was unsuccessful, and Papineau lived out the remainder of his days in exile in France.

In Upper Canada (present-day Southern Ontario), many had grown disgusted with the colony's governance, as well as the practice of favoring and granting land to British settlers over any settlers with American origins or ties. Inspired by the unrest in Lower Canada, a Scottish-born Canadian named William Mackenzie led a group of his followers in an attempt to seize the colonial government and establish a republic. Each time the insurgents met with the loyalist militia, they were easily scattered, and Mackenzie himself eventually sought shelter in the United States. However, the United States was interested in liberating Upper Canada from the British Crown and supported Mackenzie and his followers as they executed a series of raids on Upper Canada throughout 1838. Mackenzie's rebellion eventually faltered, and after spending years in exile in New York, he was granted amnesty by the Canadian government in 1849.

With many rebels executed or deported to the penal colony in Australia, the British government realized that they were dangerously close to losing control in Canada. Lord Durham was sent to assess the situation and advise the British government on the most sensible way forward. The resulting 1841 Durham Report recommended that Upper and Lower Canada be united into one colony (to force assimilation between the Anglo and French-Canadians) and urged for the implementation of responsible government in the region. The British government unified Upper and Lower Canada into the Province of Canada with the 1841 Act of Union and set up a parliament that had equal representation from both Upper and Lower Canada. This was a step in the direction of a responsible government, but Canada would have to wait for six more years to win self-government on a local level.

Durham's forced assimilation of French and Anglo-Canadians made him a hated figure in French-Canadian circles, and in 1867, the Province of Canada was redivided into Quebec and Ontario. Yet his observations and report were crucial in the long road towards Canadian self-government.

CANADA ON THE WORLD'S STAGE (1842-1918)

After the difficult loss of their American colonies in 1783, Great Britain kept a tight grip on their remaining North American strongholds in Canada. However, as the nineteenth century dragged onward, the desire to expand and grow the empire into Asia, particularly India, significantly cut back on British attention paid to Canada. With Canadian politicians largely left to their own devices, discussions cropped up suggesting that all of Britain's holdings in North America be merged and united under one colonial government. Inspired by the laws and organization of their southern neighbor, but also keen to avoid American missteps--the American Civil War (1861-1865) was occurring at this time--Canadians began to formulate one united Candian government. A single federal government with a parliament and a prime minister was formed, but each colony (now a province) was expected to elect a local prime minister and parliament as well. The federal government would manage things like defense, trade, and immigration while the provincial governments retained control over local matters like housing and education.

At the Charlottetown Conference of 1864, a Canadian Constitution was drafted and approved by Canadian politicians. The British government sanctioned the new confederation on July 1, 1867. With the British North America Act of 1867, Great Britain formally recognized the colonial confederation known as the Dominion of Canada. It contained the newly split provinces of Quebec and Ontario, as well as New Brunswick and Nova Scotia; the capital was established in the city of Ottawa in Ontario. Though July 1 is celebrated as Canada Day, the day Canada became a country, that is not quite accurate. Canada was indeed a largely self-sufficient dominion, but London still controlled aspects of the laws and regulations of the country through a resident British governor-general.

Canada's new government gained a larger portion of responsibilities and freedoms in the transition from colony to dominion, and the new prime minister, John

MacDonald, was keen to expand Canada's territory and power. His vision for the future of the nation included the incorporation of Britain's vast territories to the north and south in the Dominion of Canada, so that the nation stretched from Atlantic to Pacific. To increase immigration to these areas and achieve his goal, he championed the building of a vast, transcontinental railroad known as the Canadian Pacific Railroad (CPR). As the final few decades of the nineteenth century dawned, MacDonald's dream slowly became a reality. Manitoba, a large prairie province, joined the confederation in 1870, with the Pacific Coast colony of British Columbia following a year later. Prince Edward Island on Canada's eastern coast became the seventh province in 1873. Meanwhile, the steadily dwindling fur trade had forced Hudson's Bay Company to cede control of its northern territories to MacDonald in 1870. The aptly named North-West Territory had the eighth and ninth provinces, Alberta and Saskatchewan, respectively, carved out of it in 1905.

This steady expansion did not come without growing pains. In the late 1860s and early 70s, in response to both the Hudson's Bay Company handing Rupert's Land over to Canada and the increasing Canadian presence in the Red River Colony (located in the province of Manitoba), the charismatic Métis leader Louis Riel led the Red River Resistance. Riel and his Métis followers and First Nations allies occupied Upper Fort Garry in the Red River Colony, hoping to block the land transfer and secure protection for the First Nations and Métis people living in the area. The resistance failed, and the Hudson's Bay Company ceded the land while Riel fled to the United States.

The prairies of Canada remained in a place of general unrest and unease between the First Nations, Métis, and their new white neighbors. In 1871, the crown signed a treaty with the Ojibwa and Cree First Nations that handed large portions of First Nations land over to Canada in exchange for agricultural equipment and schools. Later the same year, the crown signed another treaty with the Chippewa that handed large swaths of Manitoba over to the Canadian government. The introduction of larger and larger populations to the plains of Canada was slowly destroying the ways of life for both the First Nations and Métis people. The disappearance of the fur trade in the region had stolen the jobs the Métis had relied on for generations, while the presence of larger populations and accompanying farms put a strain on the local bison population and broke up the traditional hunting and grazing lands that the Plains First Nations and Métis needed to feed themselves and their families.

This rapid and terrifying change in addition to the lack of protection afforded to them by the Canadian government left the First Nations and Métis alone and isolated. In 1884, Louis Riel returned from the United States hoping to organize all the affected people in Canada's northwest to unite and take their cause before Prime Minister MacDonald. As the new government continued to fail them, Riel formed a provisional Métis government with himself as the president. By 1885, anticipating a Canadian response, the now armed Métis resistance occupied Duck Lake and defeated the combined police and citizen forces, compelling them into a retreat and driving them out of nearby Fort Carlton.

Although Riel and his supporters didn't pursue the force they repulsed or occupy the fort, the government in Ottawa had already deployed military forces out to the plains to quash the North-West Resistance. Drawing from the small professional Canadian force as well as local militias, roughly five thousand soldiers eventually descended on the region over the course of a month. Riel's victory at Duck Lake had inspired similar uprisings to the west, with a band of Plains Cree and Assiniboine First Nations forming a war party near Frog Lake. Many settlers in the area crowded into Fort Battleford even though the leader of the war party, Chief Mistahimaskwa (Big Bear) actively tried to discourage violence. Unfortunately, a war chief named Kapapamahchakwew (Wandering Spirit) shot and killed federal Indian Agent Thomas Quinn. Several other settlers were killed by members of the war party following their war chief's example.

Though the Canadian troops had initially planned to stay in one group and take on Riel's contingent, the killings at Frog Lake forced the Canadian commander, General Frederick Middleton, to divide his forces, sending a group under William Otter to confront the combined Cree and Assiniboine First Nations near Frog Lake. Though the Indigenous fighters had early success at Fish Creek and Cut Knife Creek, the Canadian soldiers ground down the uprising at the Battle of Batoche and subsequent skirmishes. Louis Riel was captured, tried, and hanged for treason in November of 1885.

Though Macdonald's dream of Canada stretching from sea to sea was complete, it had been achieved at the expense of the people who had first called the land home. In the years that followed the North-West Resistance, the Canadian government continued to steadily erode the lives and cultures of the First Nations, Métis, and Inuit through overt means of violence and extermination and more insidious measures like the Residential School System. Children were forcibly removed from their communities and coerced into learning white cultural systems and beliefs while leaving their native cultures and families behind. Many, many innocent children died at the hands of these so-called schools. Though these sins of the past are often papered over and sanitized, Canada is only now beginning to acknowledge the truth.

Canada's newly acquired massive parcels of land were incredibly attractive to immigrants, and the early days of the twentieth century saw an uptick in the immigrant population of Canada, particularly Europeans. Though it was quickly becoming a modern and industrialized nation with a booming economy, Canada was sharply reminded of its duties to its mother nation of England when World War I (1914-1918) broke out in 1914. The fighting was far from Canada's doorstep, but England required Canada's men for its defense. Anglo-Canadians tended to be more supportive of the war effort, with French-Canadians remaining largely discontented by the endeavors to support an "English war." Even the prime minister, though overtly approving of the war, was annoyed by the seemingly entitled British demands for troops.

Nevertheless, Canadian soldiers proved themselves to be indispensable and heroic fighters throughout the Great War, particularly at the Battle of Vimy Ridge

(1917) where over three thousand Canadians lost their lives. This intense and painful sacrifice called England's control over Canada into question, and Canadians back home felt that they should be recognized as a nation completely in their own right.

6

WHAT IS AND WHAT IS TO COME
(1919-2021)

In the aftermath of World War I, many of Great Britain's colonial domains, particularly those with a white majority, began to petition for increased independence. In 1926, Great Britain, economically damaged from the war and aware of the changing world, declared that all dominions were now "equal in status," relinquishing any remaining subjugation. Canada pushed back, demanding greater legal independence, and in 1931, the Statue of Westminster abdicated Great Britain's abilities to make any laws for Canada. The British Empire was reconstructed into a commonwealth that maintained former colonies' allegiance to the British monarch, but for all intents and purposes, the countries were now fully autonomous from Britain. Canada retains its membership in the

British Commonwealth, and Queen Elizabeth II is still featured on the Canadian Dollar.

Canada suffered, as did most of the world, during the Great Depression of the 1930s. Poverty in the cities was accompanied by poverty in rural communities, and a massive drought in the Great Plains provinces turned previously fertile land into a barren dust bowl that devastated the agricultural sector.

Towards the end of the decade, Great Britain declared war on Adolf Hitler's Germany, and Canada readily entered the fray a week later. World War II (1939-1945) was the first war where Canada's troops operated under Canadian command, but once again, French-Canadians dubbed the war an "English" conflict and railed against the national draft. Japanese-Canadians found themselves alienated and victim to horrific racism, with the Canadian government's establishment of Japanese internment camps in 1942. Though a formal apology was issued in 1988, the question remains, why were Japanese-Canadians deemed a threat while German-Canadians were largely ignored? To put it simply, Canada's, much like the United States, consistent fear and othering of nonwhite populations has induced much unnecessary destruction and harm over the years.

The mobilization required for Canada to go to war successfully pulled the nation out of the mire of economic depression, and the subsequent discovery of oil in the province of Alberta helped to propel Canada into an economic boom for much of the mid-twentieth century. The wealthy young country continued to come into its own as Newfoundland joined Canada as the tenth province, and in 1965, the Union Jack was finally lowered with the introduction of the wholly Canadian Maple Leaf flag.

Though Canada had readily joined the United States' North Atlantic Treaty Organization (NATO) to combat the spread of communism during the Cold War Era (1941-1991) and had allowed the storage of US nuclear arms in the country during the 1960s, Canada strove to differentiate itself from its brash southern neighbor, framing itself as a more moderate and diplomatic world power. It achieved this recognition with Canada's refusal to join the United States in the quagmire of Vietnam (1955-1975).

Internally, the age-old conflict between Anglo and French-Canadians cropped up once more. The French Canadian province of Quebec began to see agitation for separation from Canada throughout the 1960s. Radical separatists in Quebec--the Front de Libération du Québec--bombed government institutions and other important buildings, like the Montreal Stock Exchange in 1969. Separatists were elected to the Quebec government in the 1970s, and even held a referendum on separation in 1980. The referendum was unsuccessful, but it introduced a new, increasingly cautious relationship between Quebec and the rest of the nation.

Prime Minister and Quebec native Pierre Trudeau believed that much of the rancor between French Canada and the rest of the country could be solved with the adoption of a new constitution. In 1982, the Charter of Rights and Freedoms established the civil rights of Canadians, protecting the right to freedom of religion, speech, and movement. The document also proclaimed Canada as a bilingual nation, protecting the rights of citizens to speak either English or French. Furthermore, England had retained constitutional power over Canada, but after the approval of the Charter of Rights and Freedoms, the British Parliament released its last remaining power over Canada, giving the nation control over its own constitutional laws.

Quebec refused to sign the new constitution and held yet another referendum on separation in 1995. This too, failed, but only by a narrow margin. To date, Quebec has never signed the document, though discussions of separation from Canada have been largely overshadowed by other issues in the twenty-first century.

Swept up in the tidal wave of fear and mistrust that marked the beginning of the twenty-first century, Canada entered into the War on Terror after the September 11, 2001 attacks on the United States. This engagement became the longest war in Candian history, with Canadian troops finally leaving the Middle East in 2014. Despite early refusal to join United States President George W. Bush in his expansion of the war into Iraq, Canada has remained nominally involved via airstrikes in Iraq and Syria to combat the rising threat of ISIS. More recently, Prime Minister Justin Trudeau (the son of former Prime Minister Pierre Trudeau) has pivoted to offer Canadian help in training anti-ISIS factions.

Now, like the rest of humanity, Canada faces the challenges of a changing world. Globalization and technological development have caused income inequality in the nation with a widening gulf between wealthy and poor Canadians. Increased immigration to Canada has greatly diversified the nation, but the changing demographic has sparked internal tension and fear as Canadians from different backgrounds learn to live alongside one another. Finally, the specter of climate change must be faced. As a nation that built much of its prosperity from petroleum, how can Canada fight climate change without destroying its own economy?

Canada is a stunningly beautiful country with a favorable international reputation. However, it has borne witness to and participated in great injustices on a national level. The steadfast refusal of the First Nations, Métis, and Inuit to disappear and assimilate massively contributed to Canada's past, present, and future, while its blended English and French ancestry has woven a bifurcated identity that is uniquely Canadian. Out of many intersecting cultures and ensuing clashes, a strong nation was born. So what is Canada? Who is Canadian? These questions will continue to change and develop as the years progress, but if the past is any indication, whichever culture or people walks the fertile lands or lands on the rocky shores will leave impactful footprints behind.

PRAISE FOR DOMINIC HAYNES

I hope you enjoyed this book. If you did, I'd appreciate it if you left a review on Amazon. Your reviews are the lifeblood of my business and I incorporate the feedback into future books.

To leave a review, go to:
Amazon.com/review/create-review?
&asin=B099QQZS3Y
Or scan with your camera:

OTHER BOOKS BY DOMINIC HAYNES

(AVAILABLE ON AMAZON & AUDIBLE)

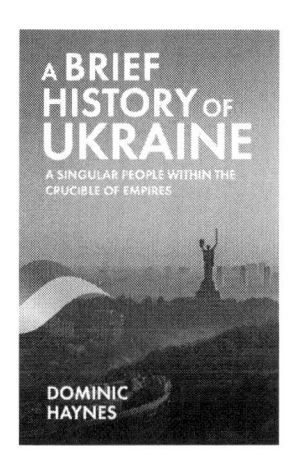

A Brief History of Ukraine: A Singular People Within the Crucible of Empires

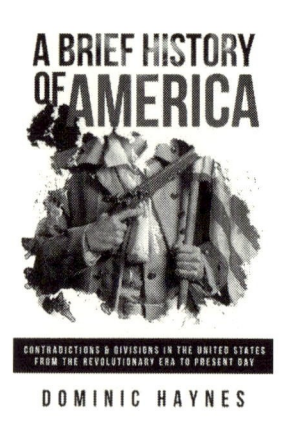

A Brief History of America: Contradictions & Divisions in the United States from the Revolutionary Era to the Present Day

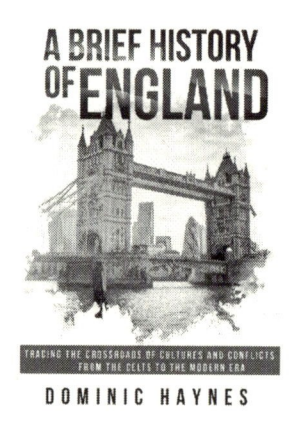

A Brief History of England: Tracing the Crossroads of Cultures and Conflicts from the Celts to the Modern Era

REFERENCES

Baker, J. (2021, January 15). Origins of the Haudenosaunee (Iroquois) Confederacy. World History Encyclopedia. https://www.worldhistory.org/article/1656/origins-of-the-haudenosaunee-iroquois-confederacy/

Beal, B. and Macleod, R. (2019, July 30). North-West Rebellion. The Canadian Encyclopedia. https://www.thecanadianencyclopedia.ca/en/article/north-west-rebellion

Blakemore, E. (2018, August 29). Canada's Long, Gradual Road to Independence. History. https://www.history.com/news/canada-independence-from-britain-france-war-of-1812

Bonikowsky, L.N. (2015, March 4). Cupids, Newfoundland: Canada's First English Settlement. The Canadian Encyclopedia. https://www.thecanadianencyclopedia.ca/en/article/canadas-first-english-settlement-feature

Bonikowsky, L.N. (2015, March 24). Laura Secord. The Canadian Encyclopedia. https://www.thecanadianencyclopedia.ca/en/article/laura-secord

Brooks, R.B. (2018, June 10). Who Fought in the French and Indian War?. History of Massachusetts. https://historyofmassachusetts.org/who-fought-french-indian-war/

Cippola, C. (2021, February 24). Vikings in Canada. Royal Ontario Museum. https://www.rom.on.ca/en/collections-research/magazine/vikings-in-canada

Editors, T. (2020, September 17). French and Indian War. History. https://www.history.com/topics/native-american-history/french-and-indian-war

Editors, T. (2019, October 9). John Cabot. History. https://www.history.com/topics/exploration/john-cabot

Facing History and Facing Ourselves. (n.d.). Stolen Lives: The Indigenous Peoples of Canada and the Indian Residential Schools.

https://www.facinghistory.org/stolen-lives-indigenous-peoples-canada-and-indian-residential-schools

First Nations in Canada. (2017, May 2). Government of Canada. https://www.rcaanc-cirnac.gc.ca/eng/1307460755710/1536862806124

Foot, R. and McIntosh, A. (2019, October 4). Rebellions of 1837-38. The Canadian Encyclopedia. https://www.thecanadianencyclopedia.ca/en/article/rebellions-of-1837

Freeman, M.A. (2020, September 24). Inuit. The Canadian Encyclopedia. https://www.thecanadianencyclopedia.ca/en/article/inuit

Gaudry, A. (2019, September 11). Métis. The Canadian Encyclopedia. https://www.thecanadianencyclopedia.ca/en/article/metis

Handwerk, B. (2019, June 5). Ancient DNA Reveals Complex Story of Human Migration Between Siberia and North America. The Smithsonian Magazine. https://www.smithsonianmag.com/science-nature/ancient-dna-reveals-complex-story-human-migration-between-siberia-and-north-america-180972356/

Hiller, J.K. (2004, August). Portuguese Explorers. Heritage: Newfoundland and Labrador. https://www.heritage.nf.ca/articles/exploration/portuguese.php

Indigenous Contributions to the War of 1812. (2016, June 3). Government of Canada. https://www.rcaanc-cirnac.gc.ca/eng/1338906261900/1607905474266

Indigenous People of Canada. (2021). Canada Guide. https://thecanadaguide.com/basics/aboriginals/

Krueger, R. R., Morton, William Lewis, Hall, Roger D., Bercuson, David J. and Nicholson, Norman L. (2021, June 29). Canada. Encyclopedia Britannica. https://www.britannica.com/place/Canada

Leiser, M. (2019, July 24). Study Reveals Vikings Might Have Stayed in Canada Longer Than Expected. Radio Canada International. https://www.rcinet.ca/en/2019/07/24/study-reveals-vikings-might-have-stayed-in-canada-longer-than-expected/

Linden, E. (2004, December). The Vikings: A Memorable Visit to America. Smithsonian Magazine. https://www.smithsonianmag.-

com/history/the-vikings-a-memorable-visit-to-america-98090935/

Mark, J.J. (2020, October 19). European Colonization of the Americas. World History Encyclopedia. https://www.worldhistory.org/European_Colonization_of_the_Americas/

Marsh, J.H. (2015, July 15). Acadian Expulsion (the Great Upheaval). The Canadian Encyclopedia. https://www.thecanadianencyclopedia.ca/en/article/the-deportation-of-the-acadians-feature

Mills, D. (2019, November 6). Durham Report. The Canadian Encyclopedia. https://thecanadianencyclopedia.ca/en/article/durham-report

Montaigne, F. (2020, January/February). The Fertile Shore. The Smithsonian Magazine. https://www.smithsonianmag.com/science-nature/how-humans-came-to-americas-180973739/

Morgan, E.S. (2009, October). Columbus' Confusion About the New World. Smithsonian Magazine. https://www.smithsonianmag.com/travel/columbus-confusion-about-the-new-world-140132422/

Morrison, D.A. (2015, March 4). The North West Company, 1779-1821. https://www.thecanadianencyclopedia.ca/en/article/the-north-west-company-17791821-feature

Nicholson, N.L. (2016, July 21). Convention of 1818. The Candian Encyclopedia. https://www.thecanadianencyclopedia.ca/en/article/convention-of-1818

Ogilvy, J.A. (2017, September 21). War of Spanish Succession. The Canadian Encyclopedia. https://www.thecanadianencyclopedia.ca/en/article/war-of-the-spanish-succession

Other Migration Theories – Bering Land Bridge National Preserve. (2017, February 22). National Park Service. https://www.nps.gov/bela/learn/historyculture/other-migration-theories.htm

Pannekoek, F. (2016, September 13). Mistahimaskwa (Big Bear). The Canadian Encyclopedia. https://www.thecanadianencyclopedia.ca/en/article/big-bear

Ray, A.J. (2020, October 8). Hudson's Bay Company. The Canadian

Encyclopedia. https://www.thecanadianencyclopedia.ca/en/article/hudsons-bay-company

Red River Colony: Timeline. (n.d.). The Canadian Encyclopedia. https://www.thecanadianencyclopedia.ca/en/timeline/red-river-colony

Reese, W. (2018, September 9). Canada's First Nations. History Today. 68 (9). https://www.historytoday.com/history-matters/canada%E2%80%99s-first-natioNs

Ridler, J. (2015, March 4). Battle of Beaver Dams. The Canadian Encyclopedia. https://www.thecanadianencyclopedia.ca/en/article/battle-of-beaver-dams

Sprague, D.N. (2015, June 19). Rush-Bagot Agreement. The Canadian Encyclopedia. https://www.thecanadianencyclopedia.ca/en/article/rush-bagot-agreement

Starowicz, M. (Executive Producer). (2000-2001). Canada: A People's History [TV Series]. CBC Television.The Métis. (n.d.). Canada's First Peoples. https://www.firstpeoplesofcanada.com/fp_metis/fp_metis8.html

The North West Company. (n.d.). Hudson's Bay Company History Foundation. https://www.hbcheritage.ca/history/acquisitions/the-north-west-company

The University of Ottawa. (n.d.). Compendium of Language Management in Canada: Linguistic History, The Linguistic History of Canada.https://www.uottawa.ca/clmc/linguistic-history/arrival-europeans

19th Century Canadian History. (2021). Canada Guide. https://thecanadaguide.com/history/the-19th-century/

20th Century Canadian History. (2021). Canada Guide. https://thecanadaguide.com/history/the-20th-century/

21st Century Canadian History. (2021). Canada Guide. https://thecanadaguide.com/history/the-21st-century/

Made in the USA
Middletown, DE
25 May 2023